Our Senses
Sight

Kay Woodward

HODDER
Wayland

an imprint of Hodder Children's Books

Our Senses
Hearing ● Sight ● Smell ● Taste ● Touch

For more information on this series and other Hodder Wayland titles,
go to www.hodderwayland.co.uk

Senses – Sight

Copyright © 2005 Hodder Wayland
First published in 2005 by Hodder Wayland,
an imprint of Hodder Children's Books.

Commissioning Editor: Victoria Brooker
Consultant: Carol Ballard
Book Designer: Jane Hawkins

British Library Cataloguing in Publication Data
Woodward, Kay
   Sight. - (Our Senses)
   1.Vision - Juvenile literature
   I.Title
   612.8'4

ISBN 0750245980

Printed in China by WKT Company Ltd

Hodder Children's Books
A division of Hodder Headline Limited
338 Euston Road, London NW1 3BH

Cover: A boy snorkelling so he can see
fish underwater.

Picture Acknowledgements
The publisher would like to thank the following for permission to reproduce their pictures: Archie Miles 12; Ardea 19 (Jim Zipp); Corbis 4 (Tom & Dee Ann McCarthy), 7 (Royalty-Free), 9 (Earl & Nazima Kowall), 11 (FK Photo), *Imprint page* and 13 (Jack Hollingsworth), 14 (Ariel Skelley), 21 (Gallo Images/Anthony Bannister); FLPA 20 (B B Casals); Getty Images *Cover* (The Image Bank/Pete Atkinson), *Title page* (Stone/Patrisha Thomson), 8 (Taxi/David Leahy), 10 (Stone/Pascal Crapet); Martyn F. Chillmaid 16, 17; NaturePl.com 18 (Lynn M. Stone/ Royalty-Free); Wayland Picture Library 5, 15. The artwork on page 6 is by Peter Bull and the artwork on pages 22-23 is by Jane Hawkins.

Contents

Words in **bold** can be found in the glossary on page 24.

Look around!

The world is filled with colours and shapes. Some things move and some things stay still. Some things are light and bright. Others are dull and dark.

▼ A merry-go-round is full of moving colour.

4

Our **sense** of sight allows us to see the many amazing things all around. We use our **eyes** to see.

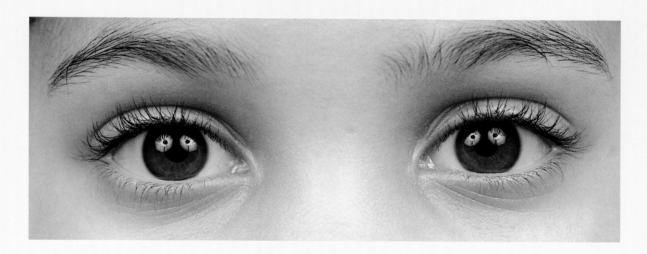

▲ The coloured part of your eye is called the **iris**. The black centre is called the pupil.

How we see

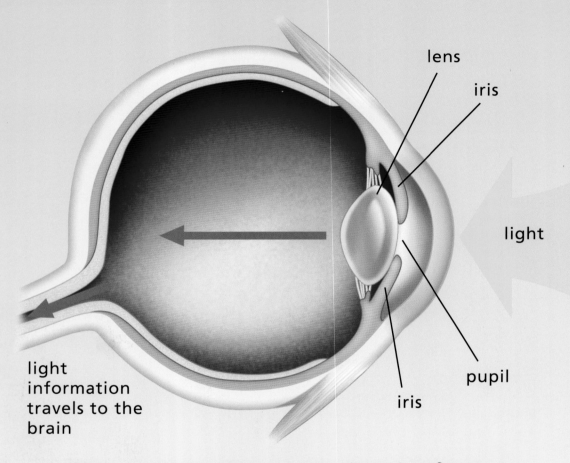

lens

iris

light

light information travels to the brain

iris

pupil

▲ This is what the eye looks like from the inside.

Information about the colour and shape of an object travels into your eyes. Your brain uses the information to form a picture. This is how you see things.

Each of our eyes gives us a slightly different view of things. Try holding an object in front of your face and then shutting your left and then your right eye. Can you see the difference?

When your brain puts the views from your two eyes together, it helps you to work out how near or far away objects are. ▼

Light and dark

▼ Pupils shrink in bright light.

Light enters your eyes through the **pupils**. Pupils change size to let the right amount of light into your eyes. In bright light, pupils shrink to stop too much light entering the eyes.

8

▲ Pupils grow bigger when it is dark.

When it is darker, pupils grow much bigger. This lets more light into the eyes so that the person can see better.

Tears and blinking

Tear ducts are tiny holes near the corner of each eye. Tears leak out of these holes when we are upset.

We blink thousands of times
every day. Blinking keeps eyes
clean, healthy and wet.

Clear or fuzzy?

The **lens** is near the front of the eye – it helps us to see. If the lens is the right shape, things look clear. If the lens is longer, shorter, thinner or wider, things look fuzzy.

▲ clear image

▲ fuzzy image

Some people have perfect eyesight. But many people need **glasses** to help them to see clearly.

Seeing clearly

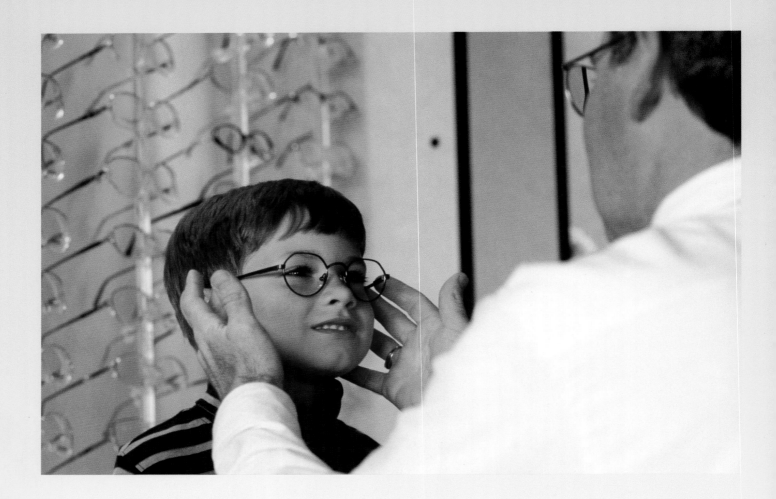

Opticians test how well people can see. They put different lenses in front of the eyes, until they find out which type of lens helps you to see better. The correct lenses are then used to make a pair of glasses.

Many people like to wear **contact lenses** instead of glasses. Contact lenses are small pieces of plastic that are placed on the surface of each eye.

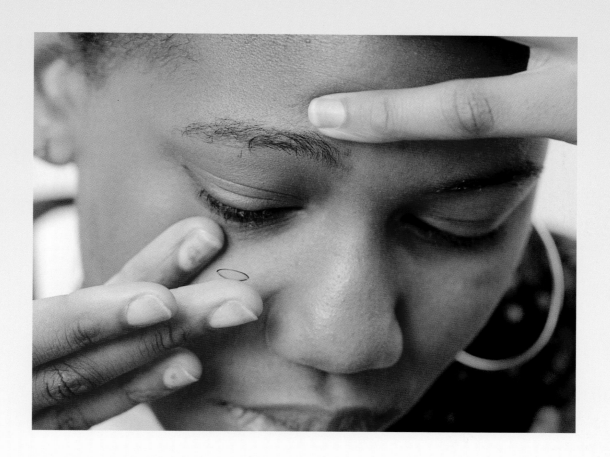

▲ Contact lenses need to be kept very clean.

Blindness

Blind people are not able to see. Blindness can happen because of an injury or an illness. Some babies are blind when they are born.

◄ Guide dogs are specially trained to help blind people.

Braille is a type of writing made up of raised
dots. Blind people read by touching the dots
with their fingers.

Animals

▲ Cats can spot the tiniest movement in the dark.

Some animals see in different ways to humans.
Many sharks can only see in black and white.
Cats' eyes are good for seeing in the dark.

▼ A hawk flies high above the ground, looking for prey.

Hawks have excellent eyesight. As they swoop through the air, these birds can spot small animals far below.

Minibeasts

Spiders have eight eyes. This means that they can see out of the back, the front and the sides of their head – all at the same time!

▲ A spider has eight eyes.

Insects, such as butterflies and dragonflies, have just two eyes. Each eye is made up of lots of smaller eyes. Information from the tiny eyes is sent to the insect's brain to form one picture.

Can you believe what you see?

Optical illusions are things that trick the eyes and brain. What do you see in the following pictures?

◀ 1. A vase or two faces?

Answer: This picture shows a vase and two faces! Can you see a light-blue vase? Look again and see if you can spot two dark-blue faces.

▼ 2. Are the purple lines bendy or straight?

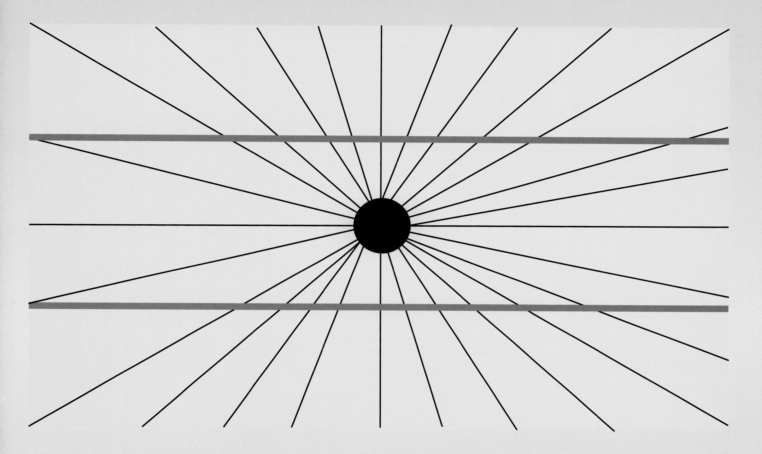

Answer: The purple lines may look as if
they are bendy, but if you hold a ruler
beside them, you'll see that they are
straight. Your eyes have been tricked by the
round, black spot and the thin, black lines.

Glossary

contact lens A small piece of plastic put on to the eye to help someone to see better.

eye The part of the head used for seeing.

glasses A pair of lenses held in front of the eyes by a frame. Glasses help people to see better.

information Things that tell you about something.

iris The coloured part of the eye.

lens A small clear object; there is a lens inside the eye.

optician Someone who tests eyes and sells glasses to help people see better.

pupil The black centre of the eye.

sense The power to see, hear, smell, feel or taste.

Index